Safe, Warm, and Snug

Stephen R. Swinburne

ILLUSTRATED BY Jose Aruego AND Ariane Dewey

Voyager Books • Harcourt, Inc.

San Diego   New York   London

www.harcourt.com

First Voyager Books edition 2002
Voyager Books is a trademark of Harcourt, Inc., registered in
the United States of America and/or other jurisdictions.

The Library of Congress has cataloged the hardcover edition as follows:
Swinburne, Stephen R.
Safe, warm, and snug/written by Stephen R. Swinburne;
illustrated by Jose Aruego and Ariane Dewey.
p. cm.
Summary: Describes how a variety of animals, including kangaroos,
cockroaches, and pythons, protect their unhatched eggs and young
offspring from predators.
1. Parental behavior in animals—Juvenile literature.
[1. Animals—Habits and behaviors.
2. Animals—Infancy.] I. Aruego, Jose, ill.
II. Dewey, Ariane, ill.   III. Title.
QL762.S84 1999
591.56'3—dc21   98-9978
ISBN 0-15-201734-8
ISBN 0-15-216378-6 pb

C E G H F D

The illustrations in this book were made with pen and ink,
gouache, watercolor, and pastel on Strathmore Kit paper.
The display type was set in Worcester Round.
The text type was set in Goudy Catalogue.
Color separations by United Graphic Pte. Ltd., Singapore
Printed and bound by Tien Wah Press, Singapore
Production supervision by Sandra Grebenar and Wendi Taylor
Designed by Lydia D'moch

For Heather, with love
—S. R. S.

For Juan
—J. A. and A. D.

Fish fry swimming tight—
Watch out! Catfish bite.
Mama cichlid opens wide . . .

Baby fish are safe inside.

When hungry dingoes stalk and hunt,
Joey hides in a pouch up front.
Kangaroo pouch is dark and deep,
Joey peeks while Mama leaps.

Crawling cockroach carries her sack,
A precious purse, hard and black.
On stormy days, under rainy sky,
Her thirty eggs stay warm and dry.

Four eggs, black and brown,
In a killdeer nest on open ground.
The killdeer drags her wing on rocks . . .

And with this trick she fools the fox.

Baby sloth hangs on her back,
As mother walks, slow and slack.
Baby clings with long curved toes,
While prowling jaguar comes and goes.

Emperor's egg sits on Papa's feet,
Kept warm and snug in snow or sleet.
Papa's belly, plump and white,
Covers his egg, day and night.

Surinam toads have holey backs,
Where eggs are hidden from all attacks.
The eggs become tadpoles where they stay . . .

And when they're toads, they hop away.

Coiled python, still as stone,
Warms her eggs, white as bone.

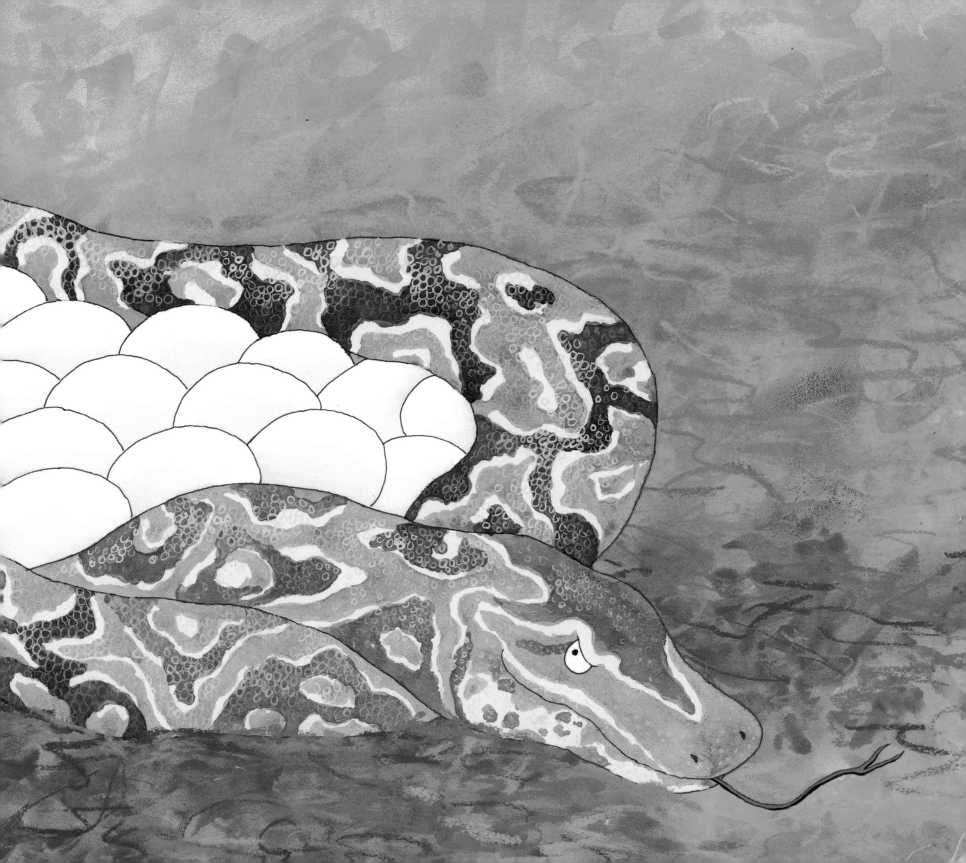

She guards her stack from storks and cats,
From lizards, turtles, and whiskered rats.

Mama sea horse puts her batch
Of eggs in Papa's pouch to hatch.

Papa broods a fishy mass,
Safe from crabs and bigmouthed bass.

Tumble beetle, tumblebug—
In a dung ball, her eggs are snug.
She rolls the ball into a hole
To keep away mouse, keep away mole.

Young bat, hold on tight—
Mama bat soars tonight.

In this furry hug, fly across the moon,
Away from owls that zip and zoom.

How Animals Protect Their Young

Cichlid

Most fish lay their eggs in the water and then leave them, providing no parental care. Small freshwater fish called cichlids release their eggs into the water, then carry them in their mouths until they develop into baby fish. The mother guards her brood until the fry can survive alone. At the first sign of danger, she signals the young to reenter her mouth, where they will be safe. Cichlids are found in many tropical countries throughout the world.

Kangaroo

A newborn kangaroo, called a joey, is about the size of a honeybee. Soon after it is born, the joey climbs through the mother's fur and into her stomach pouch, where it nurses and grows bigger. Even when a joey is large enough to run, it climbs back into the pouch when there is danger nearby. In the pouch, the joey is protected from hunting dingoes and other predators. Kangaroos live in Australia and New Guinea, Tasmania, and the Bismark islands.

Cockroach

Cockroaches are active, fast-running insects that eat almost anything—from beans to books. The female cockroach lays her eggs in a leathery capsule or purse, which she carries at the end of her body. When the eggs are ready to hatch, she deposits the case, called an ootheca (oh-uh-THEE-kah), in a safe place. Cockroaches exist throughout the world but are most common in tropical climates.

Killdeer

Killdeer are common shore-birds. They build their nests out in the open, along river-banks, in fields, or on lawns. If an animal or person gets too close to its nest, a kill-deer performs what is called the "broken wing" display: Pretending to be hurt, it drags its wing or limps and calls wildly while slowly leading the predator away from the nest. Killdeer are found throughout most of North and South America.

Sloth

Sloths are very slow-moving mammals that spend much of their lives upside down, hanging from tree limbs and eating leaves. A mother sloth cradles her baby or carries it on her back for six to nine months. In its mother's arms, a young sloth is protected from eagles and from falling to predators on the forest floor. Sloths live in the tropi-cal rainforests of Central and South America.

Emperor penguin

Winter temperatures in Antarctica sometimes drop as low as minus 94 degrees Fahrenheit. As soon as the female penguin lays her single egg, the male rolls it onto his feet and covers it with a warm fold of belly skin, protecting it from the icy environment. The female sets off to the open sea to feed. The father penguin remains in one place, in-cubating the egg for two months and living off energy from stored fat until his mate returns. Emperor penguins are found only in Antarctica.

Surinam toad

After the female Surinam toad lays her eggs, the male toad presses them into pits on her back. Each egg develops into a tadpole in its soft cup of skin. The tadpoles grow into small toads, and when they are ready, they break through the lid of skin that covers them and hop away. Surinam toads are found in Trinidad and the South American countries of Surinam, the Guianas, Brazil, Bolivia, and Peru.

African rock python

Most mother snakes leave their eggs as soon as they lay them. Snake eggs are often deposited in scooped-out hollows under flat stones. But after laying a clutch of up to one hundred eggs in a pyramid one-foot high, the female python coils herself around the pyramid. She stays curled around the eggs for two or more months, leaving only to drink water. During this incubation period, she contracts her muscles to increase her body temperature, which keeps the eggs safe and warm. The African rock python is the largest snake in Africa and exists throughout that continent.

Sea horse

Sea horses move through the water by beating their almost invisible fins. The female sea horse deposits her eggs (as many as several hundred) in a pouch on the underside of the male. The father broods, or incubates, the eggs. (Females visit their mates every morning for about twenty-one days until the young are born.) When the eggs are ready to hatch, the father squeezes his pouch and several young pop out at a time. Sea horses live in tropical oceans in the southern parts of the world.

Tumblebug

Tumblebugs, which are also called dung beetles, lay their eggs in balls of dung. When it's time to lay eggs, the male and female tumblebug form a small dung ball. Together they roll the ball to a chosen spot. The female lays her eggs inside the ball, where they will be protected from predators. Then the male and female bury the dung ball. When the eggs hatch, the beetle larvae eat their first meal: dung. Tumblebugs are found throughout the world.

Bat

Bats are the only mammals that fly. They venture out at night, using their extraordinary hearing to navigate and to locate insects to eat. Because many types of bats are born naked and helpless, a baby bat is carried by its mother, clinging to her fur as she flies in search of food. Later, as the young bat grows and becomes more independent, the mother bat leaves her offspring at a roost while she feeds. Bats are found throughout the world except in the Arctic, the Antarctic, and in the highest mountains.